Victorian Propriety

A Visual Survey of Social Invitations
used in the United Kingdom during
the Mid-Nineteenth Century

Frank A. Uhlir

Victorian Propriety
A Visual Survey of Social Invitations used in the United Kingdom during the Mid-Nineteenth Century

Copyright © 2022 by Frank A. Uhlir

All rights reserved. No part of this book may be reproduced or transmitted in any form or by any means without written permission of the author.

ISBN 978-0-9993630-0-3

Library of Congress Control Number: 2023902059

Published by: Frank A. Uhlir - Athens Georgia

Overview

This study examines a variety of invitations to social events that were utilized in the United Kingdom during the early years of the reign of Queen Victoria. The social etiquette standards that were embraced during the early years of her reign had a profound and lasting influence on the social landscape of the entire civilized world.

United Kingdom of Great Britain and Ireland

The United Kingdom of Great Britain and Ireland significantly influenced the social landscape of the entire civilized world during the early Victorian era. Queen Victoria was regarded as the most influential leader in the world during the mid-nineteenth century for maintaining very high standards for the use of proper etiquette and restraint within all formal social settings. [1]

Victoria was first addressed as Queen at the age of 18 on the night of June 20th, 1837.

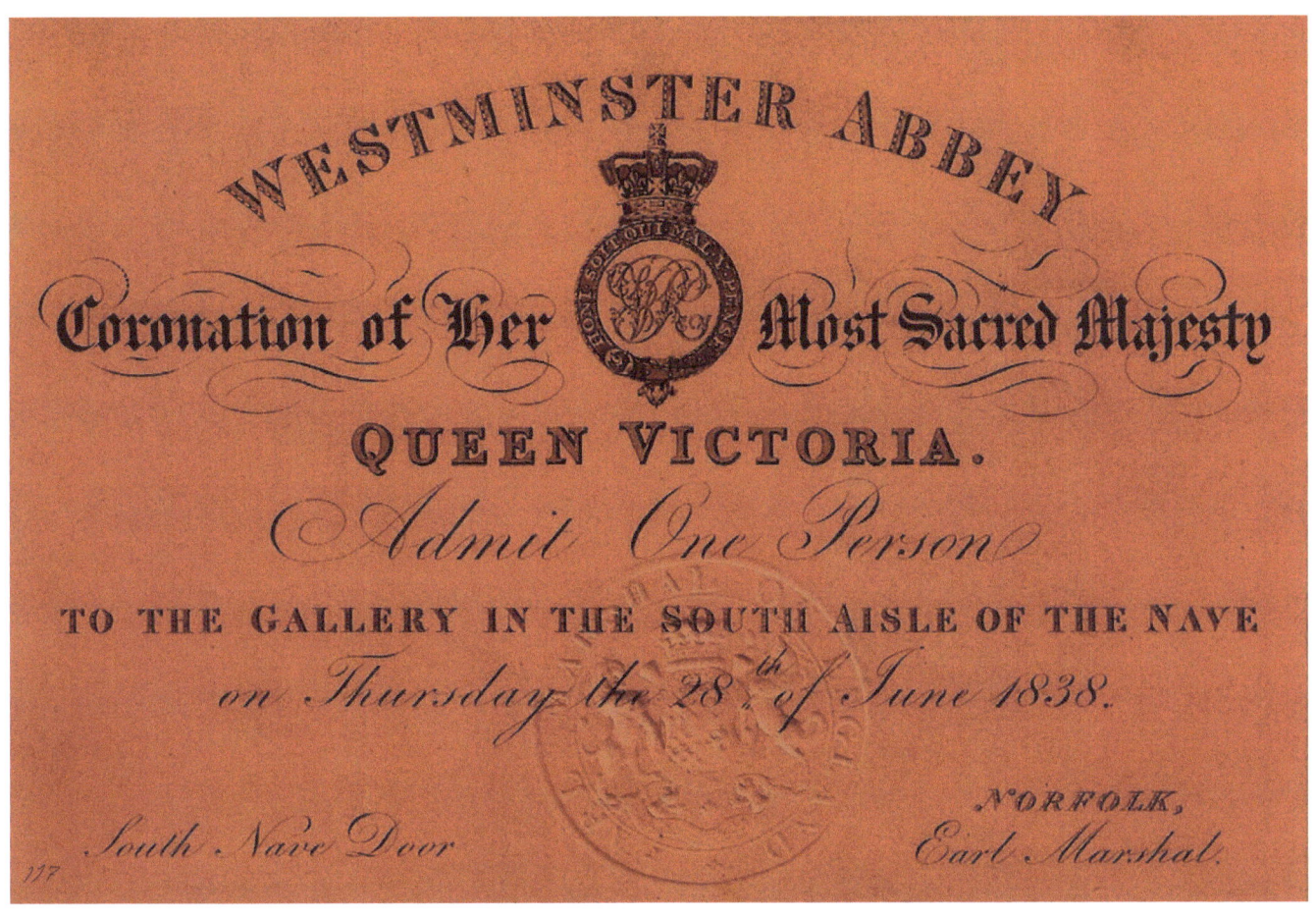

The formal coronation of Queen Victoria took place on June 28th, 1838 at Westminster Abbey. (2) The official invitations that were prepared for admittance to the coronation were all embossed with the official seal of the realm.

An engraving of young Queen Victoria dressed in a fashionable formal dress and sash.

Social events in London were often quite extravagant during the era. (3) The attire worn to fancy social engagements during the mid-nineteenth century superbly reflected the romantic, sentimental, and unsurpassed artistic aspects of the era.

During the reign of King William IV, invitations typically did not specify much about any social expectations as to what kind of clothing would be appropriate to wear to a specific social function, other than the occasional use of the term "military dress." Queen Victoria changed that trend in a somewhat dramatic fashion.

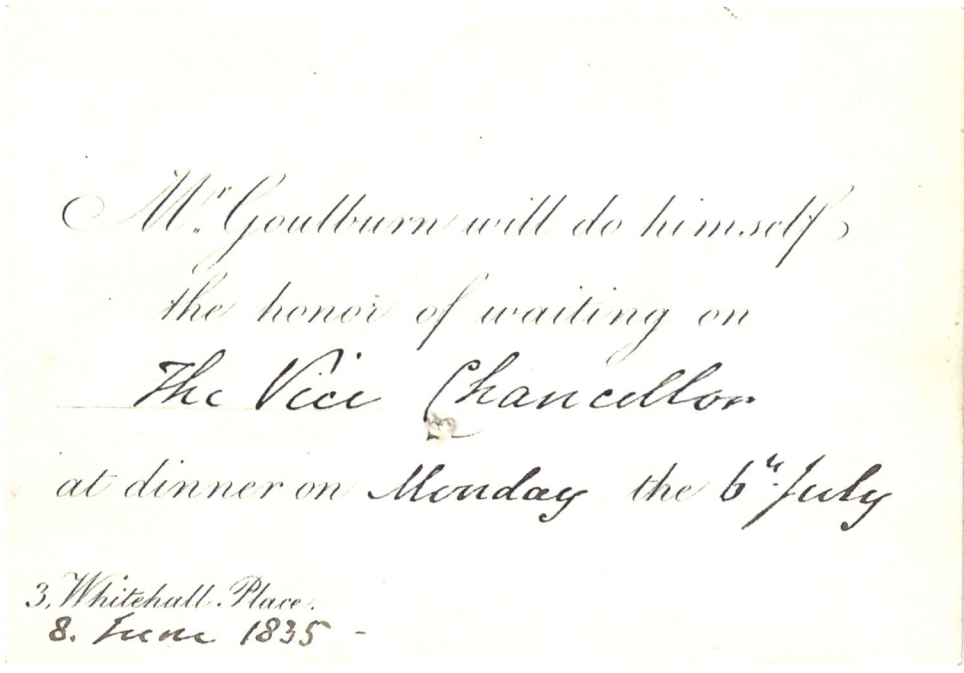

An invitation sent by Mr. Henry Goulburn that solicited the Vice Chancellor to join him for dinner at 3 Whitehall Place on Monday, July 6th, 1835.

A similar style of invitation sent by the Countess of Derby to Mr. Pakenham Alderson for a visit, at 23 St. James Square on Wednesday, June 10th, 1842. Mary, the Countess of Derby, was part of Queen Victoria's circle during her teen years.

Peerage titles that were bestowed upon people by the Royal Family were very important. Many invitations listed the title of the person without listing the name of the person.

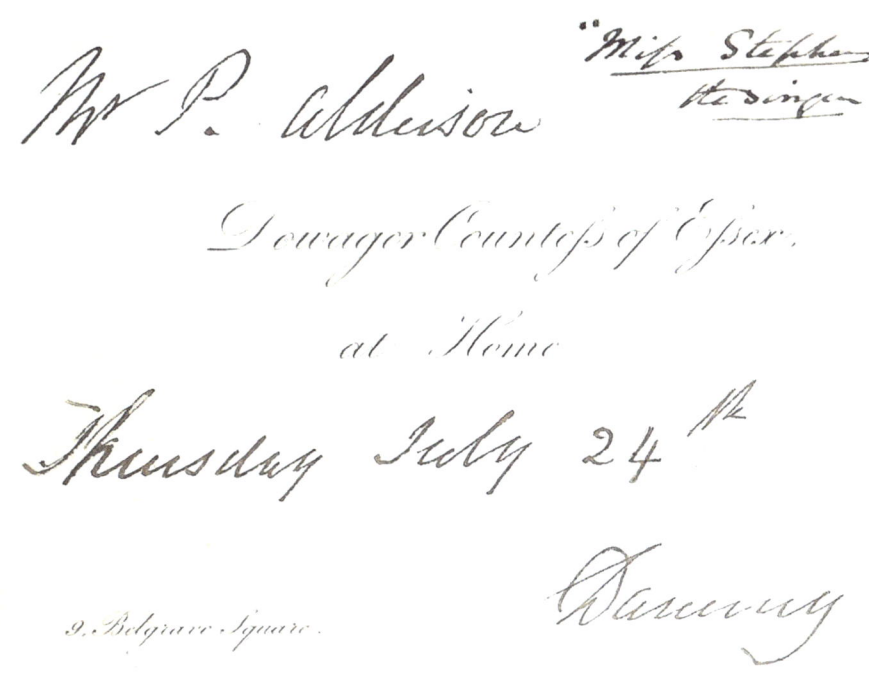

An invitation sent out by the Dowager Countess of Essex that noted "Dancing."

An elaborate invitation sent out by Kitty Stephens, the Countess Dowager of Essex. (4)

Queen Victoria was very particular about establishing very precise guidelines for proper dress within her purview. Almost all of the invitations initiated by Queen Victoria and arranged by Lord Chamberlain for social gatherings prescribed what level of dress was appropriate for the occasion. Events attended by the queen initiated social dress expectations that included notations such as Full Dress, Military Dress, Frock Dress, Promenade Dress, Morning Dress, and Hunting Dress. (4)

The Lord Chamberlain is commanded by The Queen to invite Lieut Colonel Sullivan to a Ball on Wednesday the 7th of May, 1851, at ½ past 9 o'Clock. Buckingham Palace. Full Dress.

An invitation sent by Lord Chamberlain that solicited attendance at a "Ball" held at Buckingham Palace on May 7th, 1851. Full Dress was noted, but if this lieutenant colonel was on active duty, he would have been allowed to enter wearing his regulation uniform.

Full Dress was the most formal attire worn during the period. When presented directly to Queen Victoria it was mandatory to wear white silk gloves.

The Lord Chamberlain is commanded by The Queen to invite Mr Christopher & Lady Sophia Tower & Miss Tower to a Ball on Monday the 10th of May, 1858 at ½ past 9 o'Clock.

Buckingham Palace.   *Full Dress.*

An invitation sent by Lord Chamberlain that solicited attendance at a "Ball" held at Buckingham Palace on May 10th, 1858. The invitation was addressed to the gentleman first in spite of the superior title of "Lady" with whom he would escort to the ball.

On occasion, prestigious organizations and honorable societies invited Queen Victoria to attend one of their social functions. A few attempts were made during the 1840's to assault Queen Victoria, so tight security was commonplace at events she attended. (5)

The Corporation of London request the honor of Mr. J. S. Cunningham's Company at a Ball in the Guildhall on Wednesday, the 9th of July, 1851, when Her Majesty has been graciously pleased to intimate Her intention of honoring the Corporation with Her presence.

The favor of an Answer, addressed to the Town Clerk, Guildhall, is particularly requested on or before the 2 day of July next, and if honored with acceptance a Card of Admission will be forwarded.

Guildhall.
June, 1851.

An invitation sent out by the Corporation of London that solicited attendance at a "Ball" held at Guildhall on Wednesday, July 9th, 1851. The invitation specified that, "Her Majesty has been graciously pleased to intimate Her intention of honoring the Corporation with Her presence." Because of the ongoing security concerns for the protection of Victoria, the invitation also designated: "The favor of an Answer addressed to the Town Clerk, Guildhall is particularly requested on or before the 2 day of July next, and if honored with acceptance a Card of Admission will be forwarded."

During this era, invitations were used for all kinds of social events. Because the queen prompted the standards of dress for most social activities, it was common to see a notation included on an invitation that indicated the required clothing to be worn.

> **Conversazione.**
>
> Royal Botanic Society of London.
>
> The President and Council request the Honor of Mr. J. S. Cunningham's Company to meet the Members of the several Botanical & Scientific Societies of London and to view the Gardens on Wednesday July 23rd from 1 to 5 o'Clock.
>
> J. D. C. Sowerby
> Secretary.
>
> Gardens Regents Park.
> Promenade dress.

An invitation sent by the Royal Botanic Society of London that solicited attendance to view the Gardens at Regents Park on an afternoon of Wednesday, July 23rd. The invitation specified that the occasion provided the opportunity "to meet the Members of the several Botanical and Scientific Societies of London and to view the Gardens…"

The event committee specified that Promenade Dress was to be worn.

During the Victorian era, it was commonplace for many invitations to be initiated for events held to honor new and exciting ventures. The empire was flourishing and many new economic and cultural advances were celebrated.

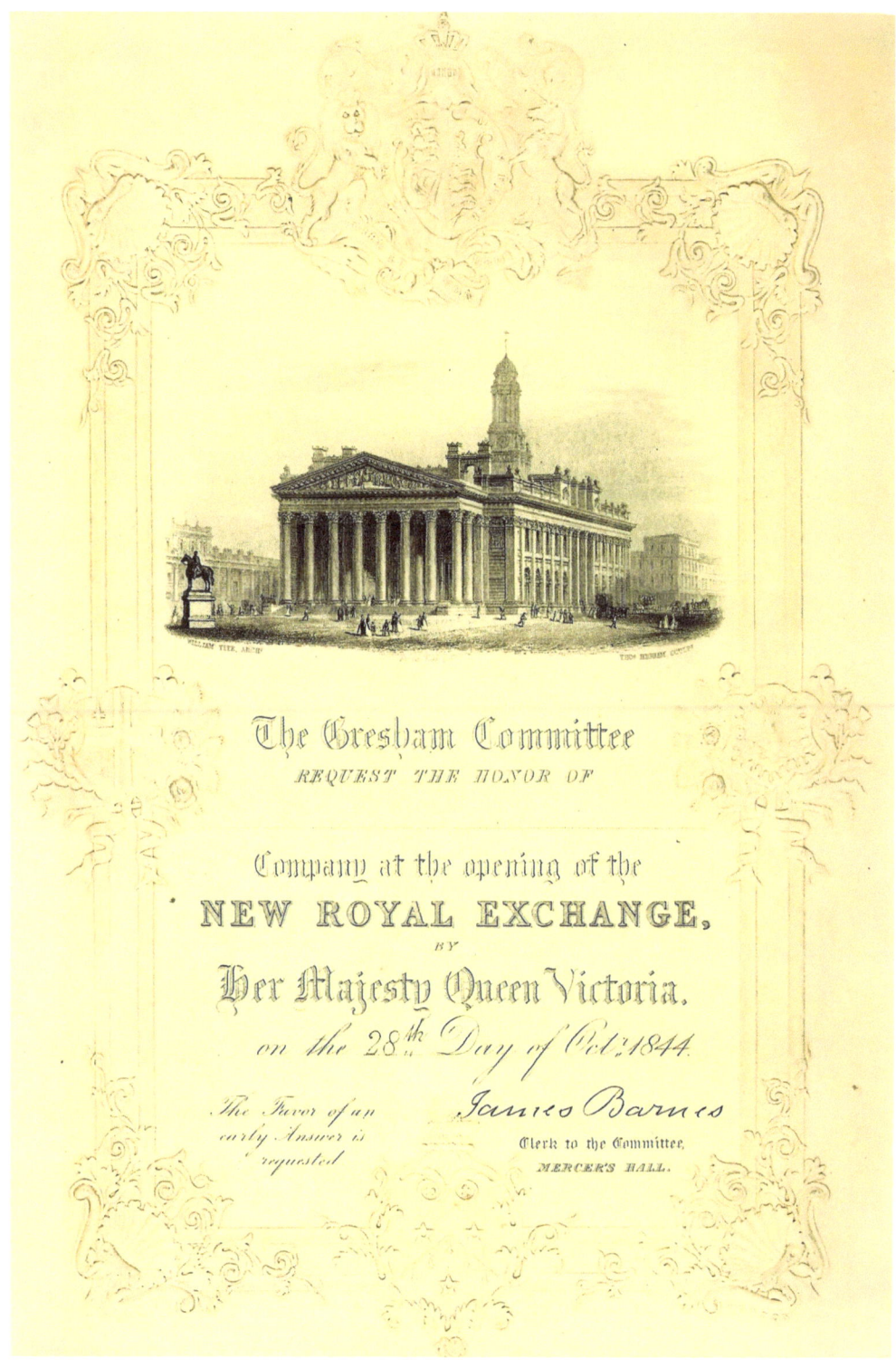

An invitation sent by the Gresham Committee that requested participation in the celebratory opening of the "New Royal Exchange" building on October 28th, 1844 in London.

Some of the invitations that emerged due to the influence of Queen Victoria were quite detailed due to the exact nature of the social event. Punctuality and an adherence to a precise schedule of planned activities and schedule of transportation were important.

An invitation sent by The Lord Mayor and Lady Mayoress that invited guests on a river excursion on the Thames River and to partake in a dinner near Twickenham.

"The Lord Mayor & Mayoress Present their Compliments to, and request the honor of Ms. Vivian's Company on board the Lord Mayor's State Barge lying off Westminster Bridge, on Saturday, the 21st day of July, 1849, at half past Eleven o'Clock precisely, to proceed to Kew and go on Board the Navigation Barge, The Maria Wood, and proceeding in her up the River off Pope's Villa, Twickenham, where they will Dine at Four o'Clock.

The Maria Wood will be at Kew Bridge until Two o'Clock, if more convenient to go on board there.

Carriages to be either at Richmond at seven, or Kew Bridge at eight o'Clock.

Mansion House, 30th, June 1849.   An Early answer will oblige.

Industrial expansion and economic growth during this era prompted the need for better organized commodity exchanges to meet the needs of the growing manufacturing sector.

A very ornate lace bordered invitation that admitted the bearer "TO THE CEREMONY OF OPENING THE NEW COAL EXCAHNGE" on Tuesday, October 30th, 1849.

While many industrial enterprises produced great wealth, most of that wealth was owned by the social elites who had little in common with the average workers of the era.

The reverse side of the Coal Exchange invitation shows an actual map of the area where the exchange was located. It displayed an area where much wealth was concentrated.

CLOTHWORKERS' COMPANY,

MONDAY, AUGUST 4, 1856.

THOMAS LEACHMAN, Esq.

Master, in the Chair.

WARDENS.

EDWARD PRITCHARD, Esq. | JOHN DORMAY, Esq.
ALFRED FRANCIS, Esq. | JOHN FAVELL, Esq.

A SELECTION OF VOCAL MUSIC,

Under the Direction of

MR. FRANCIS,

PERFORMED BY

MR. LOCKEY,   MR. YOUNG,   MR. FRANCIS,

MR. H. BUCKLAND   AND   MR. J. L. HATTON.

A program put on by the Clothworkers' Company that took place at their historic hall which served as one of the most widely known and celebrated venues in London. (6)

Guildhall was one of the oldest and certainly one of the most prestigious venues found in London proper. The core building was constructed in the 1440's. Numerous important civic and ceremonial functions were held in the grand hall during the era. (7)

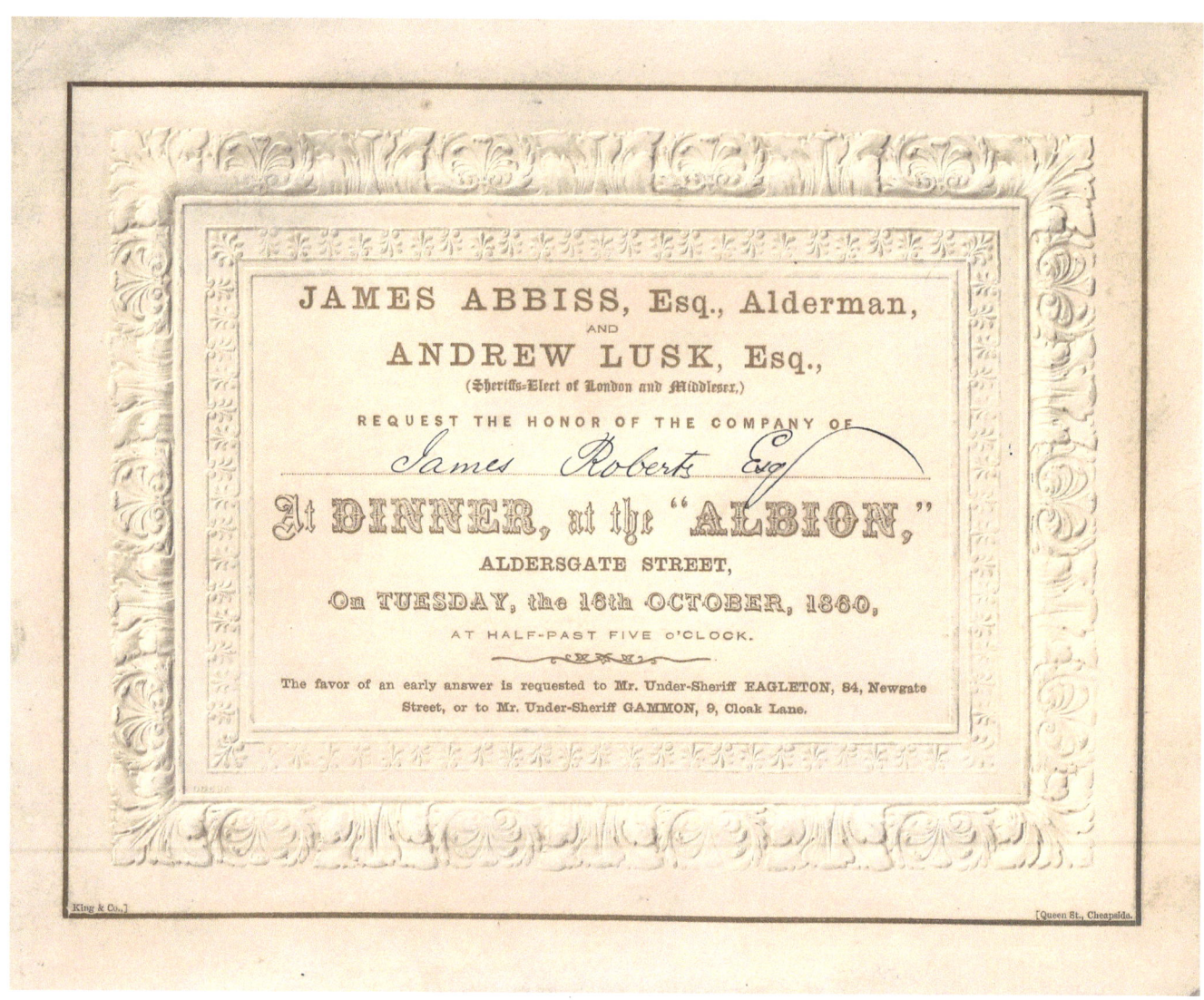

An invitation to "Dinner at the Albion" sent out to celebrate the results of a local election in London on Tuesday, October 16th, 1860. The Albion Tavern was known for its sumptuous dinners and excellent wine selection. Charles Dickens celebrated the completion of his novel "Nicholas Nickleby" at the Albion in October of 1839.

Social discourse was greatly encouraged during this era and social events were often staged to formalize the process to promote a common setting for enlightenment. This concept also provided a medium where a variety of cultural interests could be explored.

Society for the Encouragement of the Fine Arts.

The President and Council have the honor to invite Thos Walcot Esq. and Friend to a Conversazione the Portland Gallery 315. Regent St on Wednesday Evening, March 20. 1861, at Eight o'Clock.

An invitation sent by the president and council of the "Society for the Encouragement of the Fine Arts" for the purpose of holding a "Conversazione."

London also served as a repose for some weary of the political strife on the continent.

Mr Lauget is commanded by Their Royal Highnesses The Duke & Duchess d'Aumale to desire the pleasure of Mr Denham Alderton company on Wednesday July 20 at 9½ o'clock. The favor of an answer is requested. Orleans House, Twickenham.

An invitation sent by the Duke and Duchess d'Aumale who were French subjects.

While titles of nobility played a significant role to influence the social landscape of the United Kingdom, nothing surpassed the influence of the royal family. Proper etiquette and proper decorum were of utmost importance during the reign of Queen Victoria. This emphasis influenced social discourse throughout the entire civilized world.

Pomp and circumstance were the order of the day when Albert Edward, the Prince of Wales and heir to the throne, married Alexandra of Denmark on March 10, 1863. (8)

The formal royal marriage vows took place in Saint George's Chapel at Windsor Castle.

Security was tight due to the attendance of Queen Victoria, the Prince and Princess Christian of Denmark, King Leopold of the Belgians, the Crown Prince and Princess of Prussia, and other royalty from the continent. Alfred Tennyson, Charles Dickens, and Jenny Lind were among the approximate additional 400 guests.

An official invitation required for admission to the wedding ceremony held at Saint George's Chapel at Windsor Castle on Tuesday morning, March 10, 1863. The invitation specified that "Morning Dress" was the proper attire to be worn that day. As time went on, the royal couple would become well-known for their extravagant social lifestyle.

Scotland also experienced a significant amount of industrial expansion during the era. Railroad access to the region improved travel to the cities of Glasgow and Edinburgh. While the financial circumstances of the local population improved during the era, Scotland retained much of its traditional cultural identity in respect to the nature of social events that were held. As a result, social events were viewed as being more mundane in contrast to those held within the social landscape of London proper.

Union Hotel,
7th February 1844.

The Officers of the 87th Royal Irish Fusileers, and the Gentlemen of the Ball Committee, request the honor of Mr. Grant of Bright & friends Company, at the Union Hotel, on the Evening of Friday, the 16th, at half-past Nine.

The favour of an answer is requested.

An invitation that solicited attendance at a "Ball" held at the Union Hotel in Inverness, Scotland on Friday evening, February 16, 1844 at half-past nine.

Queen Victoria and Prince Albert purchased Balmoral Castle during 1852 after first leasing the property. Balmoral served as a retreat for the royal family. The grand ballroom at Balmoral was well suited for quieter and more sublime social activities. (9)

Wales was experiencing an economic expansion, especially due to the coal mining operations which helped fuel the entire United Kingdom. While mining was profitable, much of the wealth brought forth by this regional enterprise was often not returned to the local communities. Due to the Welsh and Romani language variations that were present in Wales proper, social activities were often limited in size and scope.

A

CHARITY BALL

WILL TAKE PLACE IN THE

WELLINGTON ROOM, ROYAL HOTEL,

LLANGOLLEN,

ON TUESDAY EVENING, APRIL 2, 1850,

At which the honour of your company is particularly requested.

STEWARDS.

CAPTAIN JONES, BELLAN PLACE,
CAPTAIN CLARKE, BRYNTISILIO,
A. REID, ESQ., LLANTISILIO HALL,
H. ROBERTSON, ESQ., CHESTER.

Family Tickets to admit four, £1 10s.; Gentlemen's 10s.; Ladies' 7s. 6d., (including Refreshments), may be obtained of the Hon. Secretary, Dr. Whitton, Llangollen, who will feel obliged by an early application for tickets, that proper arrangements may be made.

A GOOD QUADRILLE BAND WILL ATTEND, AND DANCING WILL COMMENCE AT NINE O'CLOCK.

An invitation sent out that solicited attendance at a "Charity Ball" held in the Wellington Room at the Royal Hotel in Llangollen on Tuesday evening, April 2, 1850. A young Queen Victoria and the Duchess of Kent were once guests at the Royal Hotel.

Ireland was fully represented in Parliament during this era. However, there was ongoing unrest regarding the desire to gain independence from the United Kingdom. In spite of the flare ups that occurred during the late 1840's, Ireland was still very much influenced by the same rules of etiquette that were ever present in the majority of the cities across the United Kingdom.

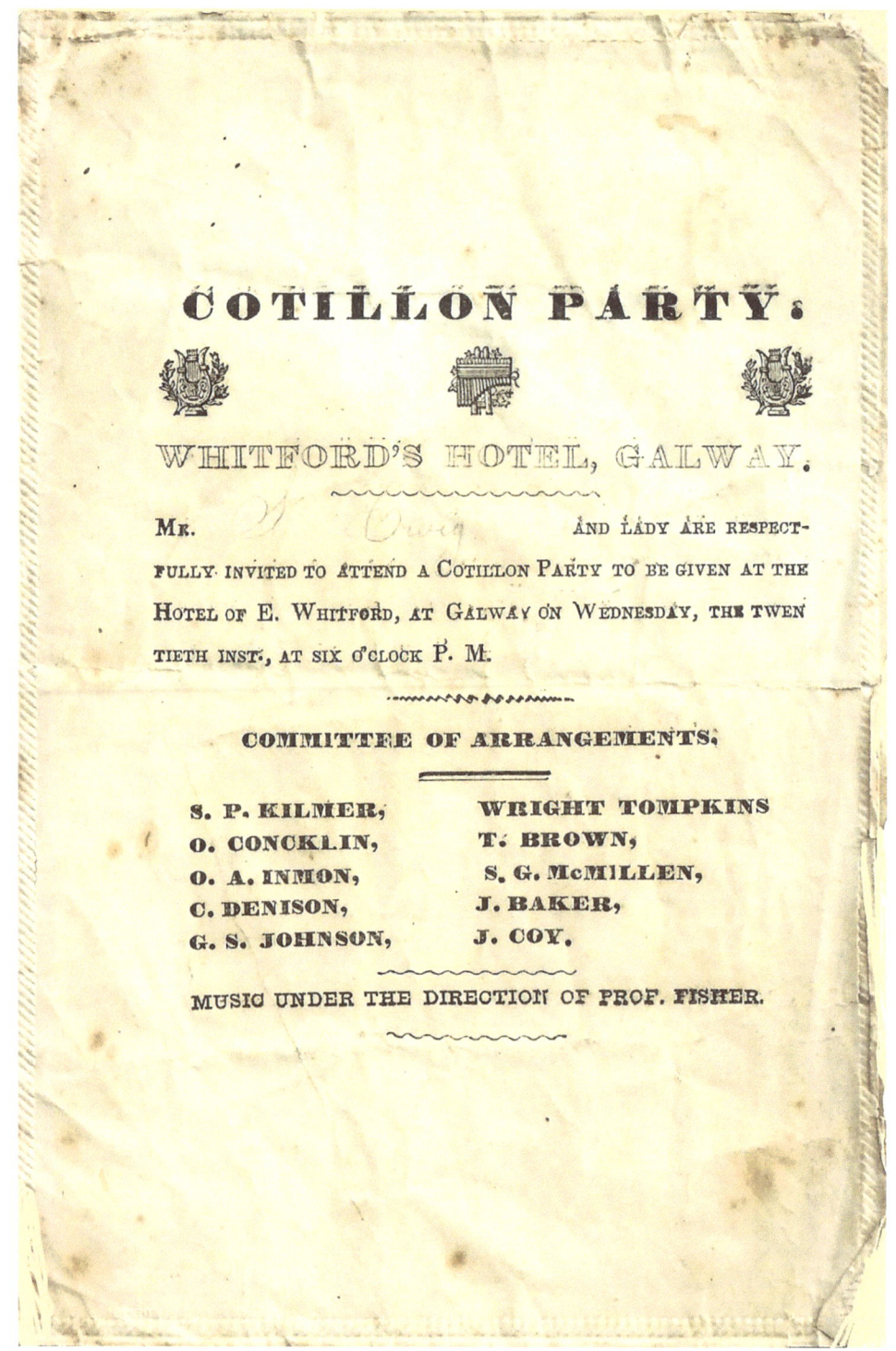

An invitation sent out that solicited attendance at a "Cotillion Party" held at Whitford's Hotel in Galway, Ireland on Wednesday, the 20th, at 6 P.M.

Endnotes

1. "Etiquette of Good Society," Cassell and Company – Limited, London, Paris, New York and Melbourne, 1860, pages 206-209.
2. *"Chronicle and Sentinel,"* Volume II, Number 82, July 31, 1838, Augusta, Georgia, page 2.
3. Jarvis, J. Albert, "Diprose's Ballroom Guide – To the Figures of the Most Fashionable Dances," John Diprose, London, 1857, pages 16-24.
4. *"The Spectator,"* Number 12, April 27, 1839, London, page 387.
5. Williams, Kate, "Becoming Queen Victoria: The Tragic Death of Princess Charlotte and The Unexpected Rise of Britain's Greatest Monarch," Ballantine Books, New York, NY, 2010, page 373.
6. *"London Evening Standard,"* October 9, 1844, London, page 1.
7. *"Illustrated London News,"* July 12, 1851, London, page 28.
8. *"Weekly Constitutionalist,"* Volume 16, Number 14, April 8, 1863, Augusta, Georgia, page 4.
9. *"Morning Post,"* May 10, 1848, London, page 3.

www.ingramcontent.com/pod-product-compliance
Lightning Source LLC
Chambersburg PA
CBHW041438010526
44118CB00002B/114